About the author

Suzi Sung isn't an internationally renowned author or *New York Times* bestseller, she hasn't climbed Mount Everest, or saved kittens from a burning building... she didn't even graduate from university!

She's your everyday girl-next-door who has a knack for pulling people out of their moments of darkness and reminding them that, even though it rains, the sky is still blue above the clouds.

Oh... she also wrote this book.

100 DAYS OF POSITIVITY, HOPE AND GROWTH

Suzi Sung

100 DAYS OF POSITIVITY, HOPE AND GROWTH

Vanguard Press

A CIP catalogue record for this title is
available from the British Library.

ISBN 978 1 784658 23 6

Vanguard Press is an imprint of
Pegasus Elliot MacKenzie Publishers Ltd.
www.pegasuspublishers.com

First Published in 2020

Vanguard Press
Sheraton House Castle Park
Cambridge England

Printed & Bound in Great Britain

Dedication

This book is dedicated to anyone out there who is feeling sad, lost or lonely and in need of a reminder of how amazing and capable they are.

Introduction

May this book pick you up when you are down, brighten up a dark day, make you laugh when you want to cry, be a hug when you are lonely and awaken you from a sleep of unhappiness.

You Have The Power To Create The Life You Want

Sounds so simple, too simple, but the truth is your life is what you make of it and we are all capable of great things.

Dreaming it is easy — believing we deserve it is the hard part.

I'm here to tell you, right here right now in this very moment, you deserve to be happy, and you deserve the things that you think will make you happy.

So believe that you can have it… and one day you will.

Once You Know What You Want, The Rest Is Easy

If you're driving in a car with no clue where you are going, taking turns in all directions, you could end up lost, or worse, back where you started.

So many of us are lost, wandering the earth doing the 'same shit, different day' and never feeling fulfilled in life.

Find out what will bring you true happiness. Once you do, jump in that car, set the Sat Nav and off you go.

Like For Like

And no, I don't mean if you like my Instagram, I'll like yours. I'm talking about the energy we put out comes back to us.

So if you're emitting a lot of negative energy into the world, be sure that it will come right back to you in circumstances that create more negativity.

Same goes for positive energy. When you're feeling really good, you attract more things that will mirror that good feeling to come to you.

Take a moment now to have a think about what energy you are sending out and what you are attracting into your life.

If you find that you're in a negative energy space, try and do something that will help to lift your mood and bring you into a more positive state of mind so that you can start attracting more of what you'd like into your life.

You're Not Okay?
That's Okay!

It's okay to not be okay at times. When you find yourself in a situation that's not making you happy and is causing you discomfort, take it as an opportunity to re-assess your life and find out what you can do to improve it.

When you find yourself feeling low, it's your body and your minds way of telling you that something isn't quite right. Deep down, a part of you will already know there's an issue and your low emotional state is your subconscious' way of telling you.

The good side to this is that once you recognise there is a problem, you can do something to fix it.

Is Your Comfort Zone Making You Uncomfortable?

Have you ever come out of a relationship and wondered what took you so long?

Or stayed in a job way longer than you should have?

Imagine you're walking down a path and you come to a fork in the road with signposts. The sign on the left says, 'Despair Dungeon' and the sign on the right says, 'Happiness Haven'.

Which road do you take?

Seems like an easy choice, yet so many of us take the road to Despair because we're afraid of what will happen if we make a change that will disrupt our current situation and take away our safety net.

In a relationship, having someone who is making you unhappy is better than being alone. If it's a job, sticking to the same thing you've known for years despite being bored and uninspired is much easier than trying something new that you might not be good at right away.

Once you are out of a situation, it is so much easier to see the facts more clearly. But when you're in it, emotions take hold and fear nestles its way in and this is what ends up keeping you in a 'comfort zone' that is no longer comforting.

You deserve all the happiness in the world, so why settle for second best?

It's JUST A Job…

I feel like some people may need to hear this.

I have had several jobs over the years and one thing every job had in common was that there was always that one employee who just HATED being there, they were miserable, they moaned every day, they made everyone else's day miserable too. These people always astounded me, and I used to think, if you hate your job so much, why don't you just leave? There cannot be so few vacancies and so few options out there that it's worth you staying in a job that makes you so depressed! If you have to work for a living don't you want to do something that doesn't cause you to be unhappy every day?

Don't suffer unnecessarily.

Find another job that makes you want to get up in the morning, because there's more to life than just work and you deserve to do something you love.

Friends Over Followers

Social media has become a bit of a popularity contest these days, people being judged based on how many followers or Facebook friends they have.

It seems that so much focus is put on how many followers you have and how many likes you have on social media that we forget about what truly matters. Real connections, real friendships, people that cry because you're crying, hurt because you're hurting and are happy for you when you are happy.

Finding people that treat you like you are family by choice are the ones that mean the most.

Ask yourself, how many of your Facebook friends or followers would actually take time out of their day to be there for you?

If You Have To Tell Him To Respect You, He Never Will

If you find yourself in a situation where you're being made to feel unworthy by a man and you have to tell him that he is not showing you respect, the chances are he's not changing anytime soon.

If he knew your value from the start, he wouldn't have crossed the line in the first place. Do you really want to be his teacher, or do you want a real gentleman?

A gentleman knows how to be respectful already — you don't have to tell him.

No Good Without The Bad

When bad things happen, it gives us a chance to appreciate good things when they come around.

If everything was always good, we would never know how to be grateful for anything. Life isn't always going to be plain sailing and sometimes we have to go through some tough times and learn lessons along the way to get to the really good stuff.

As frustrating as it can be when things aren't going well, try to look at it as an opportunity to find something good in your life and be grateful for it.

The more grateful you are for the good things you have, the more good things will come into your life.

Time Doesn't Wait For You To Start Living

Have you ever held off doing something because you wanted to do it once you were at a particular stage in life?

I used to always hold off going to certain holiday destinations because I always wanted to go with a partner and I never thought about travelling and living abroad because I didn't want to do it alone. But ten years of living like this and I realised all this time had been wasted. I hadn't been to half the places I wanted to, I hadn't really experienced much, and I was still single!

Life doesn't stop and wait for you — it keeps going, even if you decide not to. Don't waste any more of it waiting for the right time to do something. The 'right time' is right now and when you realise that you won't let another moment pass you by.

Don't Listen To The Little 'What If' Devil On Your Shoulder — He Doesn't Have Your Back

You know when you worry about a scenario, then somehow all these crazy 'what if' thoughts go running through your head and the next thing you know, the 'quick chat' your manager wants to have with you in the morning turns into you're definitely getting fired tomorrow, even though you've done nothing wrong.

Well, I call that the 'What if' devil. He's the little red horned guy sitting on your shoulder whispering sweet little 'what ifs' into your ear, causing you to lose control of your thoughts and emotions. Panic mode sets in and then your whole day is filled with nothing but these worries.

STOP.
TAKE A DEEP BREATH IN…
AND OUT…
AND AGAIN…
AND AGAIN…

Calm your mind and focus on your breath, then once your heart rate has returned to a healthy rate, take your middle finger and your thumb together and ping that devious devil off your shoulder and realise that you're overthinking and making your situation worse than it is.

How many times have you worried about something only for it to never happen?

Life is too short to waste on the 'What ifs' in the world.

People Come Into Your Life For A Season, Reason Or A Lifetime, Don't Get Them Mixed Up

Not everyone who comes into your life is meant to be there forever — some just pass through for an experience (Season), others to teach you something (Reason), and the lucky ones are there for a lifetime.

Looking back, it's easy to see why certain people came into your life and why other people left. The difficult part is realising it at the time. The trick is to learn to accept it when people exit your life suddenly and unexpectedly. The sooner you do, the quicker the reason for it reveals itself. If you spend more time than necessary to let go of what could have been and focus all your attention on how much you miss this person, you risk missing out on new and exciting opportunities.

Like they say, a new door won't open until you close the old one, so learn to close it quick and new possibilities will come rushing in.

Breathe Before You Blow

Have you ever lost your temper at something or someone and then after it, felt mortified and annoyed at yourself for getting so angry? It doesn't feel good, nor look good.

I used to have such a short fuse and would blow up over the silliest of things. Afterwards, I'd be so disappointed with my actions and dwell on how much negative energy I had put out into the universe, wasted energy.

Nowadays, whenever I am in a stressful situation and feel like I'm ready to explode, I close my eyes and take a few deep breaths to calm myself. I try to think about the situation rationally and tell myself that everything will work out, as it always has done in the past.

If you're like me, then the next time you feel like you're ready to lose your cool, try and remember a time before when you did that, how flying into a fit of rage did nothing to help the situation and that the thing you were mad about turned out to be no big deal in the end.

Taking a few deep breathes to bring yourself back to the present moment may not seem like a big deal, but if you can calm yourself down before you say something you can't take back, you'll thank yourself for it later.

The Bad Things That Happen To You Don't Define You, What You Choose To Do Next, Does

Whatever you have been through or are going through, know that the situation you are in is not the 'end of the road' for you. Instead, try looking at it like a crossroads, giving you a chance to change something that was not working for you before.

When something bad happens people can either take the situation and turn it into something good, or let the whole situation consume them until it affects every part of their life.

For example, when a relationship breaks apart, you can become consumed with hurt and anger, question 'why me?' And feel sad that everyone around you seems to have someone except you. Valuable time is wasted moping and wishing to be with someone who is not right for you.

Or, you can look at it this way — you are now free to find someone who is a right match for you, you have time to focus solely on yourself and find something other than a partner to make you happy.

How you handle and look at a situation and what you decide to do about it can greatly affect the outcome. That's why some people can make something positive come out of a negative situation and others can't. The situation is the same, but the people aren't.

We all have a choice in how to deal with certain circumstances, so choose wisely.

Make Time Or Have A Shit Time

I always seem to hear the words, "I'd love to do that, I just don't have the time."

Think about all the things you did last week. Now, how many of those things involved doing something that made you happy?

If you've just realised that in a week you don't have many moments where you've felt real joy or contentment, then maybe it's time to do something about it.

Have you ever dragged yourself to a fitness class even though you didn't feel like it and afterwards felt so amazing and so happy you did it?

Well imagine having that feeling on a regular basis.

You can, you just have to make the decision to do it. A lot of the time people use the excuse of a bad day at work to justify not doing things. You get in from a long, hard day at work, feel too stressed and exhausted to do anything that night, but the truth is you have the energy to do it. You just have to ignore the part of you that can't be bothered.

Make the time to do the things you love because if you don't, weeks, months and even years could go by without you actually enjoying any of it.

You Will Never Be A Fly On The Wall

We can spend so much time worrying about whether people like us or not and so much time trying to please everyone else that we forget about pleasing ourselves.

Stop worrying about what other people think of you. Whether it be good or bad, their opinion is just that — it's an opinion, its neither true or false. All that matters is what *you* think about yourself and whether you're happy with who you are.

You will never really know what other people think of you, so don't waste any more time stressing about.

Just Because You've Done It For A Long Time, Doesn't Mean You Have To Keep Doing It

A lot of people these days are stuck in jobs they hate or relationships they aren't truly happy in all because they have done it for so long and think they shouldn't give it up. We have this preconceived idea that if we let go of something or someone that we've invested so much time in, that somehow, it's been a waste of time.

When in reality, the real waste of time is every moment we spend in situations, jobs or relationships that no longer make us happy.

Don't think about the time you've spent on something or someone, think about how much more time you'll lose by continuing to give it to situations that don't bring you joy.

Fear and ego will always want to keep you in your comfort zone because it's safer than the unknown. But being half-happy is not worth giving up the chance to be whole-happy and the longer you spend doing something just because it easy, the less time you will have to do what you really love.

Ignore your ego and find the courage to step out of your comfort zone, because that's where the changes happen.

Don't Take Their Word For It, Look At Their Actions

Life is too short to waste on people who are not worthy of you, but sometimes it can be hard to sort the good from the bad. I have always believed that actions speak louder than words and always follow this rule when it comes to my opinion of people.

As sad as it is, there are so many people out there who will quite happily lie to your face about who they are or what they've done. The easiest way to figure out if they are who they say they are is to look at their actions.

Take dating for example. So many girls are left confused by men purely because their actions don't match their words. Girls have become so good at making up excuses for why a guy hasn't texted them back. Maybe he's busy working, maybe he's at the gym, maybe he's recovering from a hangover, maybe he's been hit by a car and broken both hands so he can't use his phone. We re-read text messages and replay conversations where the guy told us how much he liked us and how different we were compared to other girls. And while I do believe some guys out there say it and mean it, if your man is saying one thing and doing another, there's a pretty good chance he isn't quite as amazing as he's led you to believe. Most men want to impress you at the start and act out the best versions of themselves, but over time this facade can fade and if he's losing interest, his actions will show you before he tells you.

As hard as it can be to accept, if you start judging people based on how they act, rather than who they say they are, you'll find that filtering out the crap becomes a lot easier.

Which in turn makes your life a lot easier.

If You Keep Looking Back, You'll Never Move Forward

Everyone thinks about the past from time to time and that's fine, but when you start dwelling on the past it can begin to hold you back from your future. Focusing on a sad situation and letting it consume your present time means that you're not spending any time investing in your future.

When a relationship breaks down, it can be easy to focus on how much you miss the good times with that person, remember all the promises they made or all the things you said you'd do together. Whilst you're doing that, you're not actually doing anything else to promote your own well-being.

Past hurt can make us afraid to try anything new or different, and if you don't try to come out of your comfort zone, you can't progress.

When you allow this to happen you allow your past to steal your present and therefore affect your future.

Once you decide to let go of your past and the fear of it happening again, you can then start to live in the present and make way for a better future. If you keep looking back whilst you are trying to walk forward, you won't be able to see where you are going and you might never get to where you want to go.

Leave The Assumptions To The Chess Players

People who always hold onto the past have a tendency to cause unnecessary emotional distress to themselves and others.

Take this example.

Getting angry with a friend who asks you if you can recommend a nice hotel for them to stay in near your hometown. You're annoyed because the last time they asked you this question, you ended up having to call the hotel for them, book it and pick them up at the airport to drop them off. Although it would be justified for you to be angry at this person for what they did the last time, there is no reason to be mad at them now for asking a simple question, just because you assume the same thing that happened the last time will happen again.

In life you cannot always predict what another person is or isn't going to do. You can guess, based on things they have done in the past, but there is no certainty in this method. The problem with making assumptions about people and guessing what they will do is that you already feel the emotions before anything has actually happened. You play the whole scenario out in your head and the next thing you know, you're so angry when they haven't even done anything.

Unless you're a professional chess player, you don't know need to know someone else's next five moves, so save yourself the emotional torment and react only to things that are happening now and not in the past or in your head.

It's Nice To Be Nice

Have you ever had someone bump into you and when you've apologised to them out of politeness, they just give you a look and walk away?

I've had it happen to me, and let me tell you, I did not appreciate it one bit. Manners don't cost anything and it's truly a pet peeve of mine.

But now I try not to let it bother me as much because I've realised that a person's actions/reactions have very little to do with me and way more to do with them.

Imagine this. The person who didn't apologise to you when they bumped into you had just come back from the hospital. They were visiting their grandpa and just received some very bad news. They were then having to rush home to make sure their wife was okay because she was about to have a baby and they were worried about how they were going to break the news. Would you feel as annoyed at this person then? Or would you understand why apologising to you was way down on their list of priorities that day because they had more important things to deal with?

Be nice, show kindness and have patience, even when you feel it's not deserved because you never know what someone is going through at that moment in time.

If People Won't Change, Change Your Thoughts

Sometimes no matter how much you may want someone to change, even if it's for their benefit to do so, they just won't.

You could debate and argue until you are blue in the face, but until that person makes the decision to recognise where they could improve themselves, you'll never persuade them to.

Instead of suffering the torment that comes with people upsetting you and not admitting it or rectifying it, try to take a different approach in how you look at a the situation.

My family were particularly bad for telling me I needed to lose weight and their not so subtle hints really upset me. But when I tried to explain this to them and make them see that over the years they should have been teaching me to love myself for who I was rather than try to become what they thought of as acceptable, I was met with annoyance and defensiveness.

I was fighting a losing battle.

I finally realised that no matter how hard I tried to explain to them that what they were doing and had done for years was very damaging to my self-esteem, they would never understand. They even took solace in thinking they were really doing me a favour.

Rather than continue this tiring fight to change them, I decided to change my thoughts.

I started to focus more on the positive things my family did for me. And whenever they commented on my weight I learned to let it go over my head and reminded myself that I was going to do things at my own pace and not let their pressure push me over.

At the end of the day I love my family and that outweighed my need for them to change. So if you find yourself in this situation and you cannot cut these people out of your life, try and look at the situation differently and focus on the positive.

It may be difficult to do at the start, but it will make your life a lot easier in the long run.

Blaming The Universe For Your Misfortunes Won't Change Your Situation

Being mad at the world for the bad things that happen in your life can be a knee-jerk response. But your anger won't change any of it.

I have been angry at the Universe when I've been down and realised I'm not where I want to be in life just yet. But from this experience, I have learned that my anger and frustration towards my predicament doesn't change anything. I'm not any less single or more successful because of it. Good things didn't start happening to me because the Universe was like, "Okay, you're mad, let me make it up to you".

Nope, there is no compensation for the crappiness that you feel when you're looking for someone or something to blame.

So don't waste your energy being frustrated at something that cannot be controlled or changed. Take a step back and take your power back. Realise that whilst you can't turn back time, you can move forward by figuring out what you can do to make your situation improve it and go do that.

It's very easy to feel like the universe has it in for you. But the truth is, you're not the only one. We are all going through different crappy things in life and the only way to overcome this is to show the universe exactly what you're capable of and let it see how you can bounce back from this little setback.

Do You Know A Lot?
Or Do A Lot?

My brother gave me this book once and he said, "Suz, read this, it's amazing. It will change your life." Trusting my brother's opinion, I read the book and I loved it! It really did change my life in the sense that it changed my perspective on things. A few months later, I told my brother that I had finished the book and started talking about my favourite parts, asking him what he thought. At that point he revealed to me that he hadn't actually read the book himself and had only told me he had because he had heard it was amazing and he wanted me to read it. I laughed, I couldn't believe he had fooled me so easily, but I also remember being a little gutted because I wanted to talk to him about it and I couldn't.

I don't know if he ever did read the book in the end.

We have access to so much information about anything in the world and it can be downloaded to our phone within seconds, yet despite this, very few of us actually do anything with it.

You can have all the knowledge in the world, but knowing something and doing something with that knowledge are two very different things with two very different outcomes. It's up to you to decide what to do with the information that's out there.

Do You Turn Your Words Into Air Or Action?

Have you ever said that you are going to do something, but never actually followed through?

You think about doing it, you plan how to do it, you talk about doing it, but you never actually do it.

Whether it was to join the gym, visit your grandparents more often, keep in touch with friends or read a new book once a month. They all sound like pretty good things to do and also pretty manageable, but they mean nothing if you don't actually do them.

Think about New Year's resolutions, how many times on the 31st of December have you told yourself and others you're going to lose that weight, make more effort with friends, be more mindful, try new things?

It feels great when you're making the plan, you get excited about it and can't wait to start. You envision what it will feel like once you have achieved it.

But then have you ever got to the end of the year, and started a new list of resolutions, only to find that they're almost the exact same resolutions you made last year? Depressing or what!

Don't waste any more time talking about what you're going to do and just do it, otherwise your words are nothing more than just wasted breath.

Fear Can Clutter The Mind — You Can Only Conquer It When You Face It

I remember when I was learning to drive, I was visiting my dad at the weekend and he'd asked how I was getting on. I told him my lessons were going well but admitted that I didn't particularly like roundabouts. In truth, it was more than that. I was petrified. I hated them. I lacked confidence and I honestly believed I would never pass my test. I seriously considered giving up and accepting public transport as my only means of travelling.

Right away, my dad stood up, told me to grab my keys and get my shoes on — we were going out. I did as he said, as afraid of taking roundabouts as I was, an angry dad is much scarier. We ended up spending the whole night driving up and down roads with roundabouts, going back and forth, over and over again until I was no longer afraid.

By the end of the night, I had made those roundabouts my bitch!

Had it not been for my dad, I probably would still have a fear of going through roundabouts and I would not be as comfortable or confident at driving as I am today.

He made me realise that when you face your fear, you give yourself the chance to overcome it and I am so grateful because it made me tackle other things I was afraid of in a much more effective way.

Sometimes when we're afraid of doing something, we build it up to be scarier than it is, and in turn this can knock our confidence and make us question our ability. Or worse, we ignore it until it decides to resurface again later on in life. Face your fears head on and you might find that they disappear completely, leaving more room for the all good stuff.

Come Up With Enough Excuses And You'll Be Excused!

We've all done it or had it done to us. It's finally the weekend and that night out you've had planned with the girls for weeks is finally here, but there's that one friend, who can't be bothered anymore so they think of an excuse to get out of it. Cue the text, "Hi Girls, I'm not feeling well tonight, I'm not coming out." "I've spent too much this week, I can't afford it." "I don't have anything to wear so I'm not coming." "My colleagues, sister's, neighbour's, aunties cat has died and I'm feeling too sad, so I can't come out."

Now sometimes the reasons can be genuine, but it's still disappointing when that happens, or maybe you're the friend that does it. Either way, can we all agree that when this happens over and over again with the same person, it just becomes expected of them, and then over time you think, what's the point, they won't come anyway. So you stop asking.

If you're the friend it happens to and you're left disappointed all the time, stop making the effort. You're worth more than that. True friends will always make the time. But if you're that friend that makes the excuses, have a think about the people you're letting down and stop making a habit of agreeing to something you won't follow through on. Otherwise, you might find yourself on your own, on a Saturday night with no plans.

If You Love What You Do Then Work Will Never Feel Like Work

If you were to ask any elderly person what they would do more of if they could turn back time, I bet you none of them would say they wish they'd worked more.

We will spend on average 90,000 hours working in our whole lifetime. That's ten full years. Now if you already think that's a lot, you probably won't want to spend any of that time being unhappy.

If you love your job then great! I'm truly happy for you, but if you dislike it and it's making you miserable, I have to ask, is it worth it?

I know we all have bills to pay and it's not always easy to find work, but wouldn't you rather wake up in the morning and not dread the day ahead?

So many of us are taking the stresses of work home with us and we're missing out on quality time with our family and friends, which is then adding more hours onto our lifetime of work.

I spent so many years not knowing what I wanted to do and as a consequence I worked in places that made me unhappy. From lazy colleagues, unfulfilling days, mundane tasks to working for horrible managers, when I look back on how much time I wasted worrying, stressing and crying to my nearest and dearest —I think, what a waste. At the time I let it consume my whole day and night. I dreaded going in.

I couldn't enjoy anything because all I could think about was how miserable I was and yet now it's just a distant memory that makes me thankful I'm no longer working there.

What I'm saying is, stop believing that work has to be such hard work. If you are truly unhappy, do something about it. Your time and energy is too valuable to be spent doing something you don't even like, let alone love.

Don't Catch Cabin Fever

A couple of years ago, I offered to look after a family members' dogs for a few days whilst they went on holiday. I got to stay in this lovely big house with a fridge full of food and a bar full of wine. I could not have asked for more. The only thing was that the dogs didn't like long journeys in the car or being left in the house alone, so not wanting to disrupt their routine, I decided not to travel too far.

As all my friends were busy, none of them could make it over to visit so I spent most of the days on my own with the dogs. By day three, I was having a full-blown meltdown on the phone to my friend crying my eyes out about everything bad that had happened recently and feeling like I had no purpose. I was upset about my break-up, moving back home and not having a job. Even though I knew that these things were not the end of the world and I had the power to change them in time, at that precise moment, I felt like there was no hope. I am not ashamed to admit that for a split second I wished I didn't exist.

Being alone for so long with nothing but my own thoughts to keep me company magnified my negative emotions and took hold of me to the point where I felt trapped. I could see no way out. I eventually managed to calm myself down by acknowledging that I needed help and diverted my focus and attention that night to finding professional help.

Having some 'me time' and shutting yourself out from the outside world can be nice at times and even necessary. But on the other hand, you can have a little too much 'me time'.

Have you ever stayed alone in the house all day because you had to clean, study, work, recover from illness and by the end of the day felt sad, restless, depressed or lonely?

Although we can all feel these emotions at times, cabin fever can magnify them to the point where you feel like it's the end of the world.

It's no coincidence that these feelings can surface when you have had little to no interaction with the outside world.

We as humans need social interaction and a change of scenery because being on your own for too long, can greatly affect your mind frame and emotions in a negative way.

Whenever you feel like this, leave the house, get some fresh air and go for a walk, meet a friend or even go to a shop. Just getting out and changing your environment can quickly lift your energy and change your mood.

Sometimes All You Need Is A Little Outburst

When you're trying to be more positive, emotions such as anger and frustration are viewed as negative emotions and while it is not nice to feel this way, I do believe it's crucial to own these feelings and also release them.

A lot of positivity practices teach us that if we feel happy then good things happen to us and how we deal with situations can greatly affect the outcome so it is always best to be positive. Whilst this is true, I think that on some occasions, it can cause us to ignore bad emotions that we are feeling and subconsciously hold onto them, instead of addressing them.

Sometimes just owning your feelings and letting everything out can be the most positive way to handle a situation. A good rant can help you to offload those emotions from your body and allow you to feel more relaxed, rather than bottling them all up and keeping them in the back of your mind.

So if feel like you want to offload, let it out. You'll feel so much better afterwards.

Like in a yoga practice, breathe in the good and release the bad.

Oh Hindsight — It's Such A Lovely Little Kick In The Shins

Ever heard the saying, "If only I knew then what I know now?"

Well that's pretty much hindsight for you. It sucks and it's annoying wishing you could do things differently, knowing exactly how you would do them.

But the past is the past so don't beat yourself up about something you have no control over.

Be grateful you can recognise where you went wrong and use that knowledge to be a better you right now, instead of dwelling on who you were back then.

Learn to accept it and move forward. The past cannot be changed, but your future still has a chance, so focus on that.

Anger To Action

There are five stages of a break-up, denial, anger, bargaining, depression and acceptance.

My favourite part is Anger. Sounds crazy I know, but what I've found is that when I'm full of anger, I'm also full of energy and determination to avenge my heartache by becoming the best version of myself, so that, if on the off-chance I bump into the ex, he knows exactly what he's missing.

I have never actually bumped into any of my exes, but what did happen was the anger I felt became the catalyst that motivated me to stop dwelling, move on and become better than I ever was before.

It became my fuel and my energy to take my first step into moving forward. Fear is always the chain that keeps you locked up in your current situation. But when you're angry, you don't feel fear. Take the opportunity to make the most of the strength you gain from anger and break the chain.

If you're going through heartbreak, when you get to the Anger stage, don't let it consume you, turn that energy into action.

Imagine running into your ex on the street, what would you be wearing? How would you look? What would you be doing with yourself? How would you feel? What would you say to him?

Now, take a look at where you are now.

Are you there yet? Are you the person you envisioned casually bumping into you ex and being so happy and free?

No?

Then take the anger and hurt you feel, and use it to push yourself into becoming the person you envisioned, so that if you do run into your ex, it'll be just like you imagined and if you don't, your achievements will be satisfaction enough.

Turn Regret Into Resourcefulness

I always try to make sure my regrets aren't wasted. And what I mean by that is, instead of beating myself up and focusing on what could have been, I use that knowledge to figure out what could be.

It took me until I was twenty-eight years old, a trip to visit my brother in Canada to realise there was so much more to life that the little bubble I had enclosed myself in. I had never felt the urge to travel or live in another country before. I thought I was quite happy working my nine to five job, living in my little flat and going out at the weekends. It didn't even occur to me what was out there. But after living abroad and experiencing so much, I now know better. There were times when I wished I had made this realisation sooner and that I had moved abroad at a much younger age. I often wondered how different my life might have turned out. But this train of thought wasn't making me happy, if anything the opposite. So instead of dwelling on the fact that I could have done so much more if I moved away when I was younger, I made a promise to myself to never fall into the same situation again and to do everything I can now, to make sure I have no regrets moving forward.

I'm sure we all have some form of regrets in life, big or small, and whilst you'll find me say I try not to regret anything, what I really mean is that I try to turn that regret into something more useful.

Rather than dwelling on things that can't be changed, be grateful that you can actually recognise an area in your life where things could have gone better. That realisation alone can be empowering and give you the drive needed to make sure the next time an opportunity arises, you make no room for regret.

What's Scarier Than Change? Staying Exactly The Same

Imagine if someone told you that your life would be the exact same in five years' time as it is right now, how would you feel?

Pretty gutted right, even if your life is amazing right now, you wouldn't want it to be the *exact* same, because that would become boring. You'd want it to be even more amazing. But in order for that to happen, you have to do something different.

Many of us don't like change, no matter how big or small, but in order to grow and progress, we need to allow things to shift and evolve.

Changes, whether good or bad have to happen. How many people have you heard say, "If I didn't go through what I did, I wouldn't be the person I am today", even though at the time, they probably wished it wasn't happening. If nothing in your life ever changes, then you won't get the chance to grow or learn anything new.

Don't be afraid of it, there are much worst things that could happen, like waking up in Ground Hog Day.

Which Version Of You, Are You?

Are you the best that you can be?

We are all born equal as humans, but the truth of the matter is that some people are better versions of themselves than others. And I don't mean shallow qualities like looks or wealth. I mean with how they are as people and how they treat other people.

We all have a choice when it comes to the type of person we want to become.

Some like to find ways to grow and be better than they were yesterday, while others continue living just as they already are and never make room for improvement.

Being better in this case isn't something you have or don't have. It doesn't matter who you are, where you are from, what you do, or how you look, we all have the option to upgrade and become better versions of ourselves.

It all comes down to what you chose to do and who you chose to be.

So let me ask you, what type of person do you want to be?

There Is Strength In Showing 'Weakness'

I recently went through a tough period in my life and at the time, I decided I was going to be positive and I wasn't going to let it break me. I carried on with my days like nothing had happened and spoke very little about the situation to my friends. I just told them I felt fine, because I did. Or so I thought. I never let myself deal with any emotions because it was easier to ignore them. I kept myself so busy I didn't have time to think.

Little did I know that these emotions I kept hidden beneath the surface were building up bit by bit and all it would take is one bad thing to happen to me that day for them to come rushing to the surface like steam from a boiling kettle.

That day came and I broke down.

I was full of anger, sadness, fear, hopelessness, confusion, shock, anxiety and embarrassment. I felt so lost and I was a big emotional mess. I had no idea how to cope with it all.

I decided to get some help.

I went online to look for a therapist, something I'll be honest, I have never wanted to do because I didn't like the thought that I couldn't fix an issue myself. But I knew I had to do something before my emotions wore me down.

I have to say it was the best decision I made.

I am now able to recognise my emotions and process them instead of letting them all build up and spill out at the same time and I am a much stronger person for it today.

What I learned from this is that trying to be strong isn't about feeling fine after a bad situation. Sometimes admitting you are not in the best place and acknowledging the moments where you're not feeling great is stronger than showing no emotion at all. If I never had my outburst, then I wouldn't have gone to seek help from someone and without it, I don't think I would have been able to bounce back as well as I did or cope with everything I was dealing with.

In the end, surrendering to my moment of weakness is what gave me strength.

Don't ever be afraid or ashamed to seek help or be vulnerable. It's okay if you don't have everything together, all of the time. Everybody needs a little help now and again.

Find A Friend Who Will Tell You When You Have Something In Your Teeth

I mean this both literally and metaphorically.

I've made a lot of friends in my lifetime; I've also let go of a lot too. I have always found the secret to a true friendship is finding that person who has your back, even when you don't have your own.

What do I mean by that? Find a friend who will be honest with you, even if it hurts. These people truly care for your well-being and won't just tell you what you want to hear.

Fair-weather friends are the people that tell you what they think will make you happy and keep them in the good books. They don't care if you're being mean to your boyfriend, or if you're being selfish, or if your actions are going eventually cause you more pain.

They do it for an easy life.

True friends will want to help you grow, become better and make sure you go about your day with a perfect smile. They are not afraid of hurting your feelings for the greater good. So-called friends on the other hand, are the ones that let you walk about all day with pepper in your teeth.

Do You Need An AA Meeting?

By AA I mean 'Anxiety Acknowledgement' meeting.

Up until recently, I did not know I suffered from anxiety. I was aware of what anxiety was, I would get all the symptoms and think that I was feeling this way because it was the type of person I was. I never seemed to connect the dots.

But knowing this now has made a huge difference to how I deal with things. I am able to recognise the symptoms and also figure out why I am feeling this way. It's also helped me to manage stressful situations easier, because I am able to separate my feelings of anxiety from the problem and look at the issue more logically.

I want to share with you the feelings I go through in the hopes that it may help you do the same.

How I feel when I am anxious:

Butterflies in the stomach (not in a good way).

Constant worry that something bad is about to happen.

Unable to think of anything else other than what I'm worried about.

Feeling nauseous all the time.

My heart is racing and I have nervous sweats.

I have to take deep, slow breaths to try and calm my nerves but it never helps.

If you realise you are suffering from anxiety, you don't have to go through it alone. There are so many different types of support for out there.

It's okay to ask for help when you need it.

Drinking = Overthinking

When we drink alcohol, it's either to unwind, celebrate or forget. Either way, our inhibitions are lowered and as the alcohol takes over, it relaxes the body and alters our state of mind. Our receptors slow down and we become more subdued causing a euphoric state. When you are drunk, the things that worry you fade into the back of the mind until they no longer seem important.

But the next day, this comes back ten-fold and you spend the next twenty-four to forty-eight hours contemplating your life choices and focusing on the aspects of your life that are lacking. As fun as the night was, you are left with a sore head a serious bout of depression.

Now I'm not going to tell you not to drink alcohol, because, I myself know I love a drink and despite swearing I would never do it again the next day, I know I will. But if you can learn to recognise that in your hungover state, your negative thoughts and worries are only magnified due to alcohol, you'll suffer a lot less of a hangover.

Don't get hung-up on a hangover. After a couple days of recovery, you'll find that life isn't really as bad as you thought it was.

Vulnerability Isn't Weakness

So many of us mistake vulnerability for weakness. As a result, we try to block out any feelings that make us vulnerable and in turn, hide our true selves.

It is not easy to show our vulnerable side to people for fear of hurt and rejection. But if you can learn to embrace it and accept it, you will find that you can truly accept yourself. This will help you learn to form honest and longer-lasting relationships with people.

The law of attraction is always working. If you are afraid or ashamed of the things that make you feel vulnerable and have negative feelings towards them, you will attract more circumstances that emphasise these feelings.

The only way to tackle this is to fully accept that vulnerability is a part of who you are and there is no need to get rid of it.

You Wouldn't Call A Butterfly A Caterpillar

I've done things in the past that I am not proud of. When I was a child, I wasn't the nicest to some of my classmates and I was pretty mean to my little brother. I still wince when I think about what I used to say to him.

For a long time, I felt so much guilt about the things I did and I felt like such a bad person. The worst part, I couldn't change any of it. I would feel ashamed just thinking about it and beat myself up, wishing I could go back in time and undo it all.

This was neither healthy nor productive, so I made a choice.

I decided, moving forward, that I would try every day to be a good person and become better than who I was before. And whilst I can't go back and change my choices or unsay my words, I know that who I am now is a more considerate, kind, accepting person because of my past actions.

Whoever you were in the past, 'Weakling', 'Mean Girl', 'Loser', 'Bitch', 'Narcissist', you can leave her in the past. You just have to make the choice to no longer be who you were, decide to evolve and become who you want to be.

Would You Treat Your Friends The Way You Treat Yourself?

Can you imagine telling this to a friend who is going through a tough time?

"There must be something wrong with you."

"You obviously weren't attractive enough."

"You have bad luck."

"You're not good enough."

"Your life is going nowhere."

"You should be moving on much quicker than you are."

"You are worthless."

"You are hopeless."

"You don't deserve to be happy."

"You will end up alone forever."

No?

Then why would you treat yourself in this way?

It's crazy to imagine saying any of these cruel words to strangers let alone friends! Yet so many of us tell ourselves these things on a regular basis.

Give yourself a break. None of these words you tell yourself are true, they only become true if you believe them. Be kind to yourself and take this moment to think about something you like about you.

Even Therapists Need Therapy

The mind can live without the body, but the body cannot live without the mind, so make sure it is well taken care of.

Anyone, no matter how emotionally strong or aware can still suffer mentally. Most of us at some point or another can go through something that can drastically affect how we feel in a negative way, and it can be difficult to overcome that.

Having the right tools when it comes to dealing with tough situations can drastically change the outcome for the better.

Whether it's through therapy, self-help books or talking to friends, making sure you have good mental support is important.

There is no shame in needing professional guidance. I have so much respect and admiration for people who can recognise and admit when they need help in some areas of their life and actually go out and get it.

Whatever you have been through or are still going through, there is help out there, you just have to ask for it.

Judge Someone On Who They Are Today, Not Who They Were Yesterday

I used to always forgive my friends for hurtful things they've done to me because at one point or another, they were good to me. But over time, I found that it was becoming a regular occurrence. I was sacrificing my present happiness for the sake of the past.

Take this one ex-friend for example, let's call him Jack. We became friends after going on a first date and hitting it off as friends rather than romantically. I was grateful for the friendship because he introduced me to more people when I was living in a country where I didn't know anyone. We hung out a lot and would playfully poke fun at each other with back and forth banter. But over time this 'banter' became nasty. Jack would do or say things that would make me feel like the person I was wasn't good enough and try to make me feel guilty just for being me and not being more like him. When I mentioned to him later on that it had upset me, instead of apologising he brushed it off like no big deal and actually refused to acknowledge he had hurt my feelings. I dropped the conversation, but for the first time realised that he had made me feel this way before.

He would comment on Instagram posts I made. Each time saying something negative to bring me down.

He always had some reason for why what I was doing was wrong or not good enough. Everything he said to me seemed to be a put-down or an opportunity to judge my actions.

It was clear to me then that this friendship had run its course and it was time to cut ties. I ignored his messages, got on with my day and never gave it another thought, and I can honestly say, I feel so much better.

What I'm trying to say is, your friends shouldn't get away with treating you in a way that you wouldn't accept from a stranger or you wouldn't be happy with if it was happening to your friend. Just because someone has been good to you in the past, doesn't mean you have to put up with their present crap. Same goes for relationships. Don't hold on to the person they were — look at the person they have become.

If there are people in your life right now who make you feel bad more than they make you feel good, it might be time to re-evaluate the relationship.

Turn Selfishness In Selflessness

We are all guilty of being a little selfish sometimes and even though it is okay to put your needs first, how much is too much?

I had a friend who only ever got in touch when she wanted something from me. I didn't notice it until one day a received a text from said friend. When the message flashed up on my phone, I could only read the start of it. "Hey, how are you?" That's really nice of her to text, I thought, and then I opened the message and the rest read, "I was wondering if I could borrow that top you had on last week? Also, would you be able to do my hair for me this weekend when I go out?" Ahh, so that's why she's texting me, I thought, as I read the rest of the message. I felt a bit disheartened and a bit annoyed, as she has never actually got in touch just to see how I was. It made me feel like I wasn't really valued as a friend unless it was when I had something she wanted.

Whether it's only getting in touch with someone when you want something, always choosing the restaurants you want to go to, causing an argument because you don't get your way, you might not even realise you're doing it. But I guarantee that the people you do it to notice it. These little acts of selfishness might not seem like much, but you could actually be upsetting your loved ones.

On the other hand, being selfless has its rewards.

Years ago I had a friend who was in a bit of trouble and needed a place to stay. I offered right away and told her she could stay as long as she wanted. At the time, I didn't even think about it because I knew it was the right thing to do. After about a week of her staying I was starting to regret my decision (my selfish side was coming out). There wasn't anything really bad happening, but I wasn't used to living with someone. I had lost my privacy and the freedom to do whatever I wanted. I felt I had to entertain because I had a guest and I couldn't relax. But I didn't act on these feelings because I knew I wanted to help my friend out so I stuck it out.

Then one day I came home to find my flat completely spotless and the most amazing smell of dinner coming from the kitchen. My friend had cooked and cleaned while I was at work, also wrote out a little thank you card telling me how she really appreciated me putting her up and that I really helped her out. A wave of guilt came over me for even thinking those selfish thoughts and then the feeling of joy washed over me. It felt good that I could help and that completely outweighed everything else.

My point is, being selfless might be testing at times but think about how much you can help someone who is in true need. Giving up my own space for a few weeks was a small price to pay to be able to help someone who didn't even have a home.

So the next time you feel like being selfish, why don't you try being selfless instead?

Affect Or Accept,
It's Your Choice

Sometimes in life you have to deal with things that you may not like or agree with but doing so will bring yourself a lot more peace.

Some friendships can be frustrating at times, especially if you feel like you are more considerate to your friends feelings than they are to yours. Now, if this is all the time, then I say get rid and get better friends. But if you have a good friendship overall and it's just now and again that they surprise you with their lack of common decency then you have two choices in what you can do.

1. Let the things they do affect you, feel hurt and annoyed but hold it all in because you don't want to cause drama with your friends, and you know they won't understand.

2. Come to the realisation that some people just don't think the same way as you and don't feel they are being inconsiderate with their actions.

Once you accept this, you will become less affected by how they do things and you can still continue to be friends without the hurt.

It's Okay To Outgrow Your Friends

It's always sad when you drift away from friends, especially ones you have known for years. So many memories of good times and laughter.

But as we grow and mature, we change.
Just like in relationships where people grow apart, the same thing can happen with our friends.

We are all on our own individual journey and there may come a time when you realise that you and your friends have nothing in common anymore and it's time to go your separate ways.

Cherish the memories and appreciate the good times but remember that you are on your own path in life and it's okay if it's not in the same direction as the people you used to be friends with.

Don't Get Caught Up In The Fake Reality

It's so easy to get caught up in social media apps like Instagram showing the world what is popular based on how many likes a picture has. There are so many of us creating accounts and scrolling through endless pictures of 'the perfect face', 'the perfect body', 'the perfect life'. It can really distort reality and as a consequence, people are set up to fail by trying to achieve something that is impossible.

So many of these pictures have been edited using various apps made specifically to smooth out the skin, make waists look smaller and bums look bigger. There are even people out there who crop themselves into pretty holiday destinations that they've never even been to just so they can appear to be living the 'perfect life'.

These images are not real and in turn when people can't achieve these impossible goals, they turn to dangerous surgeries to get the results they're looking for or get into debt by trying to keep up with the latest trends.

What's worse is that we have celebrities endorsing quick 'weight loss' remedies, posting half-naked pictures of themselves, product in hand, talking about how much skinnier they feel after using them. The reality is that these celebrities have chefs, trainers, surgeons and editing apps to give them these figures, not that they'll admit it.

Don't be fooled by all the fake realities being put out there in the world.

All is not what it seems.

People Will Treat You The Way You Let Them

While you can't control or change how someone acts, you can decide how they treat you.

I dated a guy for over a year who was horrible to me. He was aggressive, controlling and manipulative. He chipped away at my self-esteem to the point where I felt ugly without make-up on and I took slimming tablets (provided by him) which made me shake uncontrollably and I couldn't leave the house because I felt so dizzy.

Now, it's pretty clear that this guy was no good and did not deserve me, but the only reason he could do what he did was because I let him. It came from a place of insecurity. At the time I didn't think I was worthy of anything more than him so I allowed it to happen, believing it was all I deserved in a relationship.

I know better now.

I doubt this guy will ever change, but it doesn't matter anymore because I have. He can no longer treat me the way he did because I would no longer allow it.

So I want you to know, you deserve to be treated with love, respect and kindness. If there are people in your life right now who are not behaving in this way, you can break free.

You can choose to no longer accept it.

Quality > Quantity

When I shop, I now always go for quality over quantity. I've found that I get more use out of what I buy when I love it a little more.

I use this same theory when it comes to who I give my time to. I try to make sure that the people I spend my time with are quality people and I don't waste my time on meaningless relationships or friendships that don't bring any true enjoyment to my life.

What's more valuable? Winning a popularity contest by having hundreds of Facebook friends and Instagram followers? Or having a few true friends who would drop what they are doing right then and there to give you support when you need them the most?

Choose genuine friendships over a lot of friends and real connections over one-night stands and you'll find that the time spent with these people is more fulfilling.

Taking Pride In Your Appearance Isn't Superficial

I believe that making an effort with your appearance and being pleased by what you see in the mirror isn't as egotistic as some may think.

It's no secret that when you're dressed in your best outfit, having a 'good hair day' or your make-up has been applied perfectly, you feel good.

Looking good can be a great confidence and mood booster, so make a point of trying to feel like that every day. When you don't feel like you look your best it can affect your mood, emotions, self-esteem or mindset, and as a result affect your happiness throughout the day.

Do things that make you feel content and comfortable in your own skin. It's just as important as knowing who you are.

Simply put, when you look good, you feel good.

Dress To Impress, Yourself

It's great to get compliments, but when you become reliant on someone else to tell you that you look good in order to feel good, what happens when they're not around?

How you feel about yourself will have an effect on how other people view you. This is because the universe will create circumstances based on your feelings. If you tell yourself you feel ugly, fat or undeserving, you will come across more people and situations that make you feel that way. This is why it is so important to work on self-esteem and self-development. If you can learn to feel good, truly love yourself and be content with who you are instead of looking for reassurance from other people, you won't need to rely on anyone else to make you happy.

When you value someone else's opinion over your own then you give them the power to control your emotions. Don't look to someone else to tell you that you look amazing.

Look in the mirror and realise it for yourself.

You Don't Need To Be A Mathematician To Know That If Someone's Only Giving You Fifty Per Cent When You're Giving One Hundred, That Something Doesn't Add Up

If you feel that guy isn't putting in as much effort as you into a relationship there's a good chance he's not as into the relationship as you are, and it may be time to look at other options.

Don't invest yourself in someone who isn't willing or able to do the same for you. He should want to free up time to be with you and make an effort to see you just as much as you do with him.

Whilst it can never be equally split down the middle, it should always feel fair and you should never feel like you're always the one to initiate contact or instigate a date, no matter what excuses he tells you or you tell yourself. Regardless of the reason, the fact is that this person is unwilling or unable to give you the time or effort you deserve, so they don't deserve yours in return.

It's simple math.

WHEN SOMEONE REALLY LIKES YOU

=

THEY MAKE AN EFFORT

WHEN SOMEONE IS NOT INVESTED

=

THEY DON'T MAKE THE TIME

Don't give your all to someone who is giving you nothing.

Don't Try To Fit Into The Wrong Size Shoe

Have you ever seen a pair of shoes in the sale that you love but they only have them in a size five and you're a six?

You think to yourself, I could squeeze into them, I could break them in, they might stretch. So you try them on. You manage to get them on, just, but now when you try to walk you feel like your toes are crushing together and your feet don't feel secure, they're uncomfortable, it doesn't feel good to have them on.

They just don't fit.

When we're not being ourselves, it's the same thing.

Have you ever concealed your true thoughts and feelings or changed your appearance just to please someone else because you thought that's what they wanted you to be?

When we try to be someone we're not, it's like trying on shoes that don't fit. Whether it's for a relative, friend, colleague, or even society, trying to be someone that isn't you feels uncomfortable, disingenuous, wrong somehow. This is because you're going against who you really are and you're causing resistance within yourself.

Be proud of who you are, where you have come from and don't let anyone make you feel like you need to change to be worthy or enough.

You already are everything you need to be. Be true to yourself and things will fit into place like Cinderella's foot in a glass slipper.

Spend Time With The People You Want To Become

Have you ever walked into a room and instantly felt tension? The expression "I could cut the tension with a knife" comes to mind. You can't see, touch, smell or hear it, but you know it's there because you can feel the energy surround you. Think of your friends' energies in the same way, good or bad, they will affect you.

If you surround yourself with happy, kind, positive people, chances are you will be more like that. Just like, if you hang about with negative people who are always on a downer, you'll either become more like that or you will not want to be around them anymore. This is because we absorb the energy around us, so if that energy is good, then you'll feel good and project that back out to the world. If that energy is bad, you will either become that negativity or you will want to get away from it.

Not only that, but if you surround yourself with successful, driven, hard-working people, it helps to motivate you to do the same. It stops you from becoming complacent in your life. Whereas, if you spend time with people who are lazy, unmotivated and unwilling to try new things, it will allow you think that what you're doing is enough and won't give you the drive to achieve more.

The Universe Gives You What You Need, Not What You Want

When I look back on the relationships I've had, I think I'm so glad they never worked out, even though at the time if you were to give me one wish, it would have been to end up with at least one of those guys. Crazy when I think about it now, I'm so thankful I never got what I wished for.

Why?

Because I know now that none of these people were right for me and the experiences I've had since them, could not have happened if the relationships had gone differently, even if I was heartbroken at the time. I am so grateful now for everything happening the way it did.

When something isn't right for you, even though you think it is, the universe will do what it can to remove it from your life. Whether it's not getting the job you want because there's a better job out there or your relationship ending because someone better is about to come in, these things happen for a reason.

So if right now you're wondering why you're not getting what you want, despite being positive and taking action etc., maybe it's because the universe knows better and is shaping up a more amazing path for you to follow.

When You Accept Yourself, You Don't Need The World To Accept You

There is so much pressure in the world these days to be someone other than who you are. Magazines, marketing, social media, all contribute greatly in making us feel like we're not good enough if we don't look, have or act a certain way..

There are so many negative messages being projected into the world, whether it be what shape and size you are, your sexuality, your religion, your choice in lifestyle. It can be overwhelming and make it difficult to feel like you are enough as you are.

But don't let these outside influences rain on your parade and affect how you view yourself. Believe in who you are and what you are worth. Once you do, you'll realise that you are more enough.

Get Your Priorities Straight

What do you value most?

If I asked you to make a list of ten of the most important things to you and a list of the top ten things you spend your time on, would they marry up?

Or would your actions contradict your words?

If you put family on your list of most important things, does your time list say, 'Spending time with family' on it?

If you put helping others on it, does your time list say it too?

So many of us have a clear idea of what matters to us, yet we let our day to day lives get in the way of what's really important. Make sure that whatever you choose to spend your time on, that it means something to you and brings value to your life.

And if you find that you are not doing that at the moment, it might be time to get your priorities straight.

The Simple Steps To Becoming Who You Want

Step 1. Figure out what you want or who you want to become.
Step 2. Change your behaviour.
Step 3. BOOM! You're done!

Okay, I know, this seems so overly simplified that you're probably thinking WTF! But that's the hard-hitting truth. If you want something in life that you don't have right now, then find out what it takes to get it and change your behaviours to fit in line with your goals.

Let's say, for example, you wanted to become a bodybuilder, it takes consistent training and a strict diet. Sitting at home eating pizza and drinking wine isn't going to get you there. You have to figure out what bodybuilders' typical behaviours are and adopt them until they become habit.

Sitting about and wishing for things to happen without taking the appropriate action won't get you anywhere, no matter how hard you pray for it. Things you want won't just fall in your lap, you have to align your behaviours to match your goals and keep going until you wake up and realise that you have become what you want.

Expecting Change Without Action Is Like Reading The Same Book Twice And Expecting A Different Ending

So many of us want our lives to be different, yet don't make any kind of real adjustments to our habits and routines to bring about this change.

If you find yourself unhappy at a certain point in life and you realise something has to shift, take action and do something about it.

If you have already realised this and have taken action but what you're trying isn't working and hasn't been for a while, don't be disheartened. Recognise that maybe your first idea isn't necessarily the one that works best for you and try something different. Just make sure you don't give up and go back to your old story when things get a little difficult and you're out of your comfort zone because that's where the changes will take place.

What's the worst that could happen? You try something new and give yourself a chance at getting what you want, or you continue to do the same things and get the exact same results time and time again.

It's Now Or Never

What have you always wanted to do but haven't done yet?

Is there someone you've had a crush on but haven't told them yet?

Have you promised your little brother you'll take him to the zoo but haven't yet?

What is your life ambition and are you on the right path to get to where you want to be?

If your answer is no to these questions, what are you waiting for?

Life is short and the truth is that people only seem to realise it when something bad happens.

There's no time like the present. If there is something you want to do and you haven't set a plan in motion, maybe now is the time to do so.

Because if you don't decide to do it now, you never will.

The Easiest Way To Find Out What You Want Is To Figure Out What You Don't Want

If you are struggling to figure out what you want in life, it's sometimes easier to find out what you don't like and work from there.

Deciding what you really want can feel like so much pressure and you can spend a lot of time just trying to figure it out, without ever getting started. Or even worse, you do nothing for fear of making the wrong choice and end up just sticking to what you know.

If you feel like you're getting nowhere when it comes to finding your true passion in life, try doing different things until you find what you've been looking for.

There is no rule that says you can't change your mind, so if you end up doing something new and it turns out it's not for you, then find something else you think you might like and give that a go until something sticks.

You might have to try a lot of things that you don't like, but the process of elimination is more productive than doing nothing just because you don't know where to start.

Relax About What You Don't Have Yet, Be Present, Feel Good Right Now And Good Things Will Happen

I believe in the law of attraction and whatever you put out there you attract back into your life. I know it's not everyone's cup of tea, but hey! Each to their own.

Whether you believe or not, all I can say is that when I am feeling great, I mean really, truly happy and content, right in the very moment, good things seem to happen. Whether it be getting a call about a job interview, to gaining a new client, or getting an unexpected text from a crush, these things all happened when my mind was completely focused on something else that was making me feel amazing at the time.

It is literally like the doors to endless possibilities open up and send you all the good stuff.

Feeling truly content and happy in the moment does not always come easily to people, but so far my most successful times are when I wasn't paying attention to the things I wanted in the future. I was just focused on what inspired me right then and there.

My advice to you, relax about your future, fill as much of your days, weeks and months with things that bring you true joy and the future will take care of itself.

Trust Your Gut

When going through a period of uncertainty in my life, I've looked for answers in all sorts of places, whether it be from family and friends, psychics, horoscopes, personality quizzes, tarot readers, astrology charts, you name it, I've tried it. I even almost fell for the whole, "You've been cursed with bad luck, give me $500 and I'll get rid of it for you" scam. God, I'm cringing at that. But looking back, I know deep down that I already had the answers all along.

I was looking for the easy route, the shortcut to being happy again and questioning every little thing I could have said or did to change a situation. But deep inside, despite how upset and broken I felt, I knew this situation was for the best and I would have been even unhappier in the long run. I tried to avoid doing the work I needed to to get me through my tough time, so I looked for the answers I wanted to hear from others instead of what I needed to hear from my inner voice.

Sometimes we search endlessly for answers in crazy places because we would rather believe what we want to, instead of admitting the truth to ourselves. Learn to listen to your gut and trust that it knows what's best.

Don't Let Fear Steal Your Life

At twenty-nine, I emigrated to Canada and lived there for almost two years. I'm back home now and when I tell people where I've been for the last couple of years, the conversation sometimes goes like this.

> Person: "I would love to live abroad. I've always wanted to go there."
>
> Me: "You should do it. It's an amazing experience, you'll love it."
>
> Person: "Oh I don't think that's something I could do, move to another country by myself but I would have loved to go."

Now I'd be lying if I said I wasn't scared about moving abroad and I worried that I wouldn't like it, that I mightn't get a job and that I might not make any friends.

But after my experience, I know something much scarier than any of the thoughts I had before boarding the plane. To have let my fear of the unknown rob me of one of the best experiences of my life.

Trying something new is always scary. There are always so many things to think about and so many things that could go wrong.

But have you ever thought about what could go right?

Don't let fear stop you from doing things you want to do because you could wake up one day and realise you've let life pass you by and you haven't done any of the things you've wanted to.

Needs > Wants

Isn't it ironic…?

No one wants to go to work, but they do, so many people want to go to the gym and lose weight, yet they don't.

You would think that doing something you want to do would require less effort than doing something you need to do, but it's actually the very opposite.

When you do something that you want to do, you have a choice. You can do it and get the benefits and enjoyment out of it, or you can choose not to do it and nothing much will change. But when you *need* to do something, the consequences of not doing it, are much greater.

Take your car as an example:

Everyone loves a clean car, but not everyone has a clean car.

You want to clean your car because it looks nice, it's more comfortable to sit in, it smells good. Overall it feels nicer to drive a clean car. This 'want', whilst it can bring a better feeling, doesn't have a detrimental outcome if you don't clean it. The motivation for some people isn't great enough to make them do it, therefore, it doesn't get done.

Now, you need fuel for your car — it's a necessity. Filling up your car won't make it look nice, or smell nice (unless you like the smell of petrol) or feel more comfortable to sit in. Yet I would put money on a bet that when your car needs fuel, you will make time/money to fill it up. Because if you don't, your car may break down, which could make you late for work, which wouldn't look good to your boss and cost you more money to resolve in the long run. These consequences are far greater, therefore, the motivation to do them is higher.

My point is, if you can turn your 'wants' into 'needs', you drastically increase your motivation and you have a far greater chance of achieving your goals. Because to not achieve them, yields far greater consequences.

So when you figure out what it is you want in life, turn it into a need, a must, a, "I literally will stop at nothing to achieve this because I have to." and you will drastically increase your chance of getting your goals, because the effect of not achieving them is too big a risk to your happiness.

The Right Time Is Right Now

Have you ever said to yourself you're going to start going to the gym again, but you'll go back on Monday because it's the start of the week? Then Monday comes around and you've had a hell of a weekend, so you decide not to go. By Wednesday, you say to yourself again that you'll go to the gym this Monday for sure. You know what's coming don't you? Another Monday passes and you still haven't been to the gym.

How many times have you said to yourself you'll do something on the condition that you'll start on a particular day or when you're in a certain mood to? This method is unproductive and a waste of valuable time.

The best way to start something is to just do it regardless of the time, day, weather or mood etc.

They say habits form after thirty days of continuously doing something, but if you never get started, you'll always be on day one.

Instead of waiting for the right conditions, make the right time, right now.

Your Limits Are Whatever You Set Them At

Who has lived through this scenario before?

You go to the gym and decide that you want to start running, you say to yourself that as you're starting out, ten minutes is the maximum you can run, so you set your stopwatch and monitor it closely throughout the run.

Two minutes go by… you're starting to work up a sweat.

Five minutes in… halfway there and it's getting tough.

Eight minutes pass… you're really struggling now.

Ten minutes … you just made it and no more.

Now imagine the next time you go to the gym and you cover up the clock, focus on the television or listen to some music and just run until you can't run any more.

Do you think that bang on ten minutes you will tire out like you did the first time?

Probably not. You're more likely find you've managed to run fifteen, maybe even twenty minutes or more.

Why could you run more the second time than the

first?

The answer is simple.

When you set yourself a limit, you stop yourself from exceeding it.

If you believe that you can only achieve something to a certain extent, then subconsciously you won't allow yourself to get past it. This is because exceeding it would disrupt your beliefs and mess up the projected image of you that you have unconsciously created. When you stop giving yourself limitations, you remove the subconscious barriers that restrict you from progressing beyond what you thought you were capable of.

If you can train yourself to believe that you are limitless, you can achieve anything.

Don't Let Self Doubt Be The Unwanted Guest That Never Leaves

Whenever you're trying something new or challenging, self-doubt can pop in from time to time making you question everything you're doing.

"Are you good enough?" it will ask.

"Your dreams are unrealistic," it will say.

It's so easy to listen to self-doubts negative views and give up on your dreams and aspirations, but don't believe what it has to say.

Stay focused on your goal and you will get there. Self-doubt is consequence of fear, and fear is an emotion to something that has not happened yet or may never happen. Fear only exists in the mind, if you can take charge of the thoughts that go through your head and not allow them to interfere with your what you're aiming for, you will conquer your fears and wave self-doubt goodbye.

So the next time self-doubt comes for a visit, be sure to show it the door before it sets up home in your mind and distracts you from getting to your goals.

You Can't Have Growth Without Growing Pains

Have you ever tried something new and then gave up when it got too difficult because you didn't like how you felt or you were scared you wouldn't do well?

I used to do CrossFit, this mega intense, hardcore workout that pushed you to your limits in terms of strength and fitness. When I first started, I had no real expectations for myself, I just wanted to do it. My fitness really wasn't great at the time I couldn't even do a single push-up without my arms shaking uncontrollably. It didn't bother me too much, but as time went on and I became stronger, I started to lift heavier weights and my fitness increased. This was all great except for one problem. I now felt like I had to do better each time and if I didn't do well, then it meant I wasn't progressing. That fear of failure took hold of me to the point where I ended up dreading each class I went to.

I had created this pressure for myself out of nowhere because the workouts started to get more difficult and because I had previous scores to beat. This in turn made me not want to come to class and eventually, I stopped going.

When we do new things, we reach a make or break point where the activity becomes more challenging to the point where we are pushed out of our comfort zone, unpleasant as it can be, it is a sign of growth. We can't progress without it.

So when you're feeling like things are getting difficult, try and push through it because they are only growing pains. Once you've sprouted, you'll see that the pain was not unbearable, and the rewards were well worth it.

Is Social Media Making You Unsociable?

Isn't it ironic that we have more ways than ever to connect with people, yet we've never been more disconnected?

Put your hands up if you've done this before.

You come home after a long day at work and decide to have a sit down before you prepare dinner, get changed for the gym or get ready to head out again. You take your phone out and decide to go on Instagram or Facebook for a few minutes.

The next thing you know an hour has passed in the blink of an eye and you have no idea where the time went or even what you have done.

Doesn't sound like such a big deal right? But think about how often you go on your phone during the day to scroll endlessly through videos, memes, pictures of beautiful destinations, food images, send the occasional like.

Now add up all the time, let's say it's about three hours a day, that's twenty-one hours a week, that's almost a full day you would have spent on mindless scrolling and having zero interaction with another human being (and no, someone liking your newly posted selfie doesn't count).

Now I'm not saying you should delete all your apps and never use social media ever again. I'm just saying be mindful about how much time you're spending on these apps and think about what you actually gain from it as opposed to going out and actually doing something real.

I hear people comment on a regular basis that they haven't seen their friends in a while because they're too busy or they would love to go out and do something fun if they had enough hours in the day.

But if they didn't spend as much time on their phones, laptops, Xboxes, etc., they would have a lot more time to do all the stuff they say they're too busy to do.

Success Does Not Have An Age Limit

You can be whatever, or whoever you want to be at any given time in life. All you have to do is make a start and don't listen to those little niggles of doubt in your head that say:

"I'm too old to do this now."

"If only I started this when I was younger."

"I can't change my career now, it's too late."

Whatever it is you want from life, don't let a silly thing like your date of birth hold you back, it's never too late.

You can do it!

Everyone's Idea Of Winning Is Different, So The Only Competition You Should Enter Is The One With Yourself

We've all heard the saying, "Don't compare your beginning to someone else's middle."

We are all at different stages in our lives mentally, emotionally and physically. Despite this, so many of us still compare ourselves to people who we think are more 'successful', 'attractive' or 'intelligent', but this is neither productive nor accurate.

An athlete runner who just ran ten kilometres in under fifty-two minutes might not think they are doing well because last year they ran it in forty-nine minutes. They might feel like they've lost despite coming first in the race. Compare that to someone who is in physical rehabilitation and who just managed five steps on their own, they are elated because last week they couldn't even take one. They feel like they have won the lottery.

What I am trying to say is, you can only really measure success accurately against yourself. When you compare yourself to others, you set yourself up for failure and become less appreciative of who you are and where you are in life.

Recognise the little victories in your own life and be proud of how far you have come.

How Badly Do You *Need* It?

Picture a set of balancing scales. On one side you have *'Where you are right now'* and on the other *'Where you want to be'*. You will only achieve your goals when *'Where you want to be'* outweighs *'Where you are right now'*.

In other words, you'll only get what you want, if you need it bad enough.

The only way you won't, is if you stop trying or don't have the will to start.

I have heard so many people talk about how badly they want to lose weight because their size is getting them down, yet they don't actually ever get around to joining the gym. Whatever the excuse may be, 'broke', 'too busy', 'too tired', they are all excuses. And others will go on and on about how they want to quit smoking, whilst holding a cigarette in their hand.

The truth of the matter is that these people don't see enough value in these goals to actually go and achieve them fully. They might like the idea of it, but not enough to actually go for it.

So ask yourself, does where you want to be outweigh your excuses?

Sometimes Doing Nothing Is Just As Important As Doing Something

As great as it is to be busy and productive, our minds can go into autopilot and we end up just doing things out of habit and getting no real joy from them.

Taking a couple of hours or even a day to relax and get away from the everyday hustle and bustle can help to calm the mind, relax the body and give yourself a chance to recuperate and think about the things you are grateful for in life.

If you're feeling overwhelmed by life, take some time out to relax today and bring yourself back to the present, it'll help you to rest and reset until you're feeling ready to get back to working towards your goals again.

Stop Always Asking 'What's Next?'

I am so guilty of this, being that I am probably the most impatient person in the world. I am always wondering what's next to come. I have never been able to stay 'seated' in the sense that I always need to have a new project on the go or new goal to reach. The problem with this is that I never take the time to appreciate the present moment.

When I moved to Canada, for the first nine months I really got settled, I made amazing friends, joined a dance group and I enjoyed work. But then I got back together with an ex and we began a long-distance relationship, with the plan that I would move in with him once my visa was up. Thus began the countdown to when we would be together. I wouldn't say it ruined my experience, but it definitely hindered it, in that as much as I loved where I was, I couldn't wait to move back and start our life together.

Well, as it goes, our plan didn't go to plan and I ended up back home six months earlier than expected, single, jobless, living back at home with no clue what the hell I was going to do.

I can honestly admit that I wish I had appreciated my time over there more than I did and now I'm home I'm thinking of all the things I miss and shouldn't have taken for granted.

Working towards a future is not a bad thing, but not being able to see anything but the future means you're missing out on what's going on in this very moment. Don't make the mistake I made.

Appreciate the good things that are going on in your life right now because you never know when they might change.

Give Yourself A Pat On The Back

You may not know it or believe it, but being where you are right now is an achievement.

Take a moment to reflect on how far you have come and be proud of what you have accomplished so up till now.

Whether it's getting the job you want, passing your driving test, feeling more confident, being truly honest with yourself, realising your goals or even just being able to get out of bed, acknowledge that you have made a step forward.

You might still have far to go, but don't forget how far you have come.

Clear Your Space And Clear Your Mind

I don't know about you, but I have the best night's sleep when my room is tidy and my sheets have just been changed. I wake up feeling energised and ready for the day.

A messy living space can create more busyness around you and add to an already overrun mind. Tidying up or giving your place a good clean can also help to declutter your mind and give you a clear head to deal with the important stuff.

If you ever find your mind going into overdrive and you're having trouble relaxing, try clearing up the space around you. It will give your brain a distraction from your worries and when you are all done you might find your thoughts are easier to organise.

You Can Still Find The Positives In A Negative Situation

I'm all about making changes and moving forward etc.

But sometimes things are just what they are and nothing can be done about it, however, there can still be positive outcomes despite this.

When something like this comes along in life, there's not much to do but accept, move on and direct your attention to something that can be changed. The quicker you can learn to do this, the less anxious and frustrated you'll be.

I used to find myself getting really annoyed at things like traffic jams, being on hold for too long on the phone, the girl in work not being a team player. I would get so worked up that I couldn't focus on anything else. My day would be ruined spent being annoyed over these silly things. I realised that this wasn't doing me any good. It didn't change the traffic. My call wasn't answered any quicker and the girl at work didn't get any better. So I decided that I wasn't going to waste another second on things that I could not control. Instead, I focused my attention on the things that could be, like, leaving fifteen minutes earlier than usual to beat the traffic, being prepared for a long hold time on the phone, so that if it was answered quickly then it was a bonus. And as for the girl at work, instead of focusing on her, I focused my attention on building a better working relationship with my other colleagues and on us being stronger as a team.

So you see, just because you accept a situation for what it is doesn't mean you can't find the positive in it.

People Who Try To Cast A Shadow When You're Shining Bright Are Not Your Friends

They say you find out who your real friends are when you're in trouble, but I think you can also find out when you're doing great.

The next time you have good news to share with your friends, have a closer look at how they react. Some friends will be ecstatic for you, while others will have a more subdued reaction. These are the ones to watch for. Some people cannot be happy for you because when you're doing good, they worry you'll do better than them.

These types of people are insecure and take comfort in feeling like they are superior and in some sense, doing better than you. So when that dynamic threatens to change, you find out who is just there for you when it suits them and who's really cheering you on.

It's Okay To Have A Bad Day!

Staying positive and looking for the silver lining in everything isn't always an easy task when you're going through a rough time. Whilst looking on the bright side does make a difference, some days it's just not enough.

If you're having a tough day and you want to feel sorry for yourself, scream with anger, or cry yourself to sleep, do it. Don't feel bad about it afterwards. Sometimes owning how you feel and accepting it can be just the right kind of positive action you need for the day.

You should feel better after your outburst, and if you don't, you'll be so exhausted from the screaming or crying that you can't do it anymore.

Remember, tomorrow is a new day.

You'll See The Truth When You Are Ready To

When something bad initially happens, emotions take over and logic goes right out the window. That's why it's sometimes better to have an outsider's take on things.

When we're emotional, our thoughts become irrational, which makes it more difficult to find the answers we are looking for.

Take the ending of a relationship as an example.

When it first happens, fear of being alone, fear of change, rejection, hurt, shock all take hold and it makes us miss that person all the more and question why things fell apart. But once the dust settles and our emotions are calmer, that's when logic kicks back in and we can begin to see the facts more clearly. You may realise that your ex was disrespectful, he didn't want to commit, you wanted different things. Whatever the reason, the answers were there all along, but they only became apparent once you were open to seeing them.

Think back to a time when you had a break-up, remember at the start, it was gut wrenchingly painful and you never thought you could get through it, and now you laugh and think, I can't believe I dated that guy!.

Most of the time, the truth is right in front of you, but you won't see it until you are ready to.

You're Only Too Late When You Stop Breathing

Where is your life at right now? Are you happy? Do you feel truly fulfilled? Do you like the direction you are heading in?

If the answer is yes, then amazing! Keep doing what you're doing!

But if, like so many of us, the answer is no, then let me ask you, what are you going to do about it?

It is *never* too late to make a change, make a start, turn your life around. Whatever you've been through or are going through, it won't be like this forever. You just have to know that things will improve if you put the work in. But in order for that to happen, you cannot accept the current situation as your only option.

Don't allow yourself to suffer so much pain that you forget you can be happy.

There are so many people out there that are living their dream life. Was it easy for them? No. But was it worth it?

Definitely.

What differentiates you from these people?

Absolutely nothing!

You are just as capable of going for what you

want. I believe you deserve to live the life you dream of; you just have to be willing to go for it.

No matter where you are in your life right now, it is not late to do the things you want to do.

So make like a Nike shoe and 'Just do it'.

Take It One Step At A Time

That end goal might seem like a lifetime away and that space between where you are right now to where you want you to be can be filled with fear and doubt. It can make you stop dead in your tracks, preventing you from moving forward. When you feel like this, slip on your Louboutin's and stamp out your fear and doubt one tiny step at a time. Before you know it, you're miles away from your start point and you're on top of all your little insecurities, keeping them at bay with your killer heels.

Where You Come From Doesn't Matter — It's Where You're Going That Counts

Someone who comes from a privileged background is not guaranteed success, just as someone who is from a less privileged background is not set to fail.

Success isn't determined by how you grew up or where you come from. It depends on your own drive and ambition, and how much you want to succeed in life.

If you look at famous actors, writers or successful business women for example, they don't all come from the same background. They probably struggled more than we could imagine. Some were homeless, some lived in their cars, some even contemplated suicide before their big breaks.

Hard to imagine someone with such struggles being not only able to overcome them but to also become a great success.

One thing they all had in common was determination to succeed despite all the odds and if you have that, it doesn't matter where you come from.

Live Life Like A Baby Learning To Walk

Have you ever watched a baby learning to walk?

They use whatever is around them, a couch, a table or chair leg to stand up. Once they are steady, they try to take a step and fall tumbling down, so it's back to the beginning again. They do this every day, over and over again, getting a little bit further each time, until one day, they're running about causing havoc and getting into everything around the house.

It's amazing because babies have no fear of failing. They don't give up when they can't do it right away. They don't decide to just crawl instead or walk because it's easier and they already know how. They don't question themselves or tell themselves they aren't capable.

No, they have this instinctual determination to keep going, taking each day as it comes and once they have accomplished this, they move on to the next thing they want to do without a second thought.

We all went through the same thing as babies. We all started out unable to walk or stand, with no instructions on how to do it, but we managed it. We are all born with this lack of fear and the ability to just go for it. It's in all of us, but as we grew up, along the way, we learned to be afraid, we learned have self-doubt, to question our actions, to compare ourselves to others and thus, we learned how to give up on things a lot more easily.

Sometimes our situations can seem impossible to deal with, our goals unachievable, and solutions non-existent. But just remember that you were at one point, this fearless child, with the determination and persistence to keep going until you could take that first step. You can be that child again, by letting go of the voice in your head telling you why you can't do it and unlearning the traits that cause you to give up.

If You Like Yourself, It Won't Matter If No One Else Does

We all know that we can't be everyone's cup of tea all the time and some people just won't like us for no apparent reason.

But when you come across an incident when you find out someone dislikes you it can still be a shock. You may become insecure and paranoid about how to be with people or start to question who you are as a person. There's an element of embarrassment in finding out someone doesn't like you. It's as if you feel bare.

But if you can learn to be completely happy with who you are as a person and how you treat others, then what someone else thinks about you will not matter to you, and that can be a wonderful feeling.

So get to know yourself and get to like yourself. If you find that there are things you don't like, start to make changes until you do.

Once you've mastered this, you'll find that other people's opinions of you will no longer affect you.

You Can Without A Plan

I don't know about you, but any of my life plans have worked out the way Velma's plans worked out in an episode of Scooby Doo, except in the end I didn't get to eat any Scooby snacks. For those of you who have never watched Scooby Doo, it is a cartoon about a group of kids and a dog who try to solve ghost mysteries. The 'smart one', Velma, would come up with a plan to catch the bad guy and everyone would take their places. It never ever went as planned, but they did always get their guy in the end.

What's the point to my story?

In life there is only so much that can be planned, most of the time things work out the way they're meant to, not the way you want them to.

For example, you decide, once you finish Uni, you'll get a job, travel for a year, meet the man of your dreams, buy a house, get married, have babies, grow old together and boom! Life is sorted right?

If only!

Having a plan gives you limitations and when things don't work out the way you thought, disappointment rears its ugly head and can leave you feeling deflated. When things don't work out, it doesn't mean you won't get what you want, you just might not get it the way you expected to.

So don't worry if your plan doesn't go to plan. What you have coming could work out so much better.

Stop Wishing Your Days Away, They Will Run Out

My grandpa passed away eight years ago. He woke up one day, dazed and confused, went into hospital with what we were informed was a urine infection. Little did I know at the time that he would never recover. He would spend the next four months in a psychiatric ward, confused and incoherent, slipping in and out of consciousness with no real sense of where he was or even who he was. Turns out he had had a stroke which affected his brain, hence the confused state. The condition would only worsen until eventually his organs shut down.

What I wouldn't give for just one day with him, to tell him how much I love him and appreciate all the things he did for me. To tell him that I would be fine and not to worry, to surprise him with a visit and some of those pecan pastries he loved so much.

When he was alive, I thought I had all the time in the world. It wasn't until he passed, that I realised how short life is and how things can change in an instant.

Do you ever wake up in the morning, think of the day ahead and say to yourself, "I can't wait 'til this day is over."

I know I've been guilty of it. What a way to start your day, wishing it's over before it's even begun.

We all have hard days and sometimes it can seem

like it takes all your will and energy to even get out of bed, let alone see the day through. But if you can find it in yourself to look at each day as another chance to make it a good day and appreciate who and what you have in your life, you might find your days don't seem so bad. Every day is a gift, a chance to spend with the people closest to you.

Don't waste it.

I know this isn't new information, but I think sometimes we all need a little reminder of just how precious our days are.

Make yours count.

Winning The Lottery Won't Buy You Happiness

A lot of people make the mistake of thinking that being a millionaire will make them happy, and while being financially worry-free would be an amazing feeling, having that alone isn't enough.

If it was, all the millionaires in the world would be the happiest people around, but they're not. They still go through the same heartbreaks, stresses and loneliness that we do.

The key to happiness, is fulfilment. Finding a purpose in your life, the thing that gives you that, 'get up and go' in the morning, connection with other people, new experiences, even change. Doing something that gives you meaning to your life will make you much happier than having a large bank account.

So the next time you find yourself wishing you were a millionaire, remember, real wealth can be found in other ways, and you can be truly fulfilled without a full bank account.

Stand By Your Standards

Having high standards is not a bad thing, it means you know what you want and what your worth is.

So if you ever hear someone say, "Your standards are too high, maybe you should lower them, you might meet someone then." — don't listen.

Now when I say standards, I don't mean qualities like being rich, good looking, tall, nice car, etc., because I might even tell you to lower your standards then.

I mean the stuff that's underneath all that — loyalty, kindness, respectfulness, being family orientated. Whatever your standards may be, you have them because a part of you also possesses these qualities.

When you meet someone who has these qualities that match yours, even if they don't match what you might like aesthetically, you'll find that you connect on a much deeper level because your core values are the same.

When they say opposites attract, it's not because they're different that couples are together, it's because their core values and standards are the same so the level of respect they give each other is matched.

So don't drop your expectations and settle for anything less than who you are just because the right person hasn't come along yet. If you do, you might find you are always ending up with the wrong people.

You're Not Alone

These days people say that loneliness can be just as deadly as smoking and drinking. I know what it's like to feel lonely, it's all-consuming and sometimes it can be so hard to bear, that it has me wondering, what's the point of it all? Luckily, these thoughts pass before they can cause any real harm.

But if you're reading this and you feel this loneliness right now, please know that you are not alone. This feeling will pass if you allow it to. If you ever feel like it's all too much, please reach out to someone.

You are worthy and you deserve to be happy. You deserve love and kindness and you don't have to settle for anything less. Believe you can do anything, believe you are capable, believe in yourself the way I believe in you.

You Can Always Try Again

Just because you have tried do something once and it didn't work out, doesn't mean that you can't try again. Whether it's going for that promotion, running a full marathon, buying the house you want, or starting your own business. Not getting to where you want to be in life the first time, doesn't mean you have to give up on your dreams altogether.

You have the choice to take another go at it.

The only thing stopping you is pride and ego. They are the voices in your head telling you that to try again would be stupid because you didn't manage it the first time round. This can be the same for relationships too, but I don't necessarily mean you should give a cheating ex another chance. I mean that you can always try again to have a loving relationship with someone new who makes you as happy as you were at one point with your ex, if not happier.

Most people give up on things after one bad experience, but if we all did that, I doubt the world would be as evolved as it is today. So if you feel hopeless about a situation, remember, just because you didn't get what you wanted the first time, doesn't mean you won't the second time round.

Aiming For Perfect Is Like Pointing An Arrow Towards The Sky And Expecting To Hit A Fish

Obviously, that is ridiculous, which brings us to my point.

Trying to be 'perfect' is impossible.

It doesn't exist.

If you think about it, what exactly is perfection? Everyone has a different idea of what it is, so if you're trying to be the perfect person, you would have to be a different version of yourself for each individual.

I don't know about you, but that sounds pretty exhausting.

Our imperfections are what makes us unique and special. So embrace your individuality and realise that you are 'perfect' just as you are.

A Little Bit Of Kindness Goes A Long Way

I remember years ago being on holiday with a girl from work. It was our last day and we were sitting at our hotel bar watching the television while we waited for our bus to collect us and take us to the airport.

An old gentleman began talking to me about whatever was on TV. I replied as the girl I was with rolled her eyes making it clear she didn't want to be there. I felt bad, this man was harmless and just trying to be friendly. I remember thinking, he reminds me of my grandpa and if this were him, I'd like to think a stranger would be kind to him. So I decided to continue the conversation. As we chatted more he revealed that he used to come to this hotel every year with his wife and their friends, but over the years they had all passed away and so every year he would come back to the same hotel himself to remember the good times and honour his loved ones.

I wanted to cry right there and then.

I didn't.

Instead I decided to dedicate my last couple of hours in Spain listening to the gentleman reminisce about old times with his wife and talk about what he and his friends used to get up to. You could tell he felt great joy in being able to share stories of his past. After I left it felt good to be able to do something nice for someone else and I could tell that the gentleman was grateful for the chat. It must be lonely going on holiday yourself.

Showing kindness to a stranger doesn't require a lot of effort, but that little effort can go a long way. So the next time you have a chance, try showing some kindness to a stranger.

You might just make their day.

We All have Rainy Days, But If You Carry An Umbrella, You Don't Need To Get Wet

We all get days where things are really great. You're motivated, inspired, excited and ready to go out and achieve your goals. And then you get days where motivation is non-existent. Negative thoughts invade your brain like a big rainstorm and wash away all your great ideas and plans until all you are left with is an 'I can't do it!' attitude. This isn't uncommon even for successful people. You can't ignore it and it's not always easy to stop it from happening. The key is to ride the storm and let it pass. Don't let it sweep you away from your goals and ambitions. Accept that whilst you can't change this 'emotional weather' you can have your umbrella at the ready to stop the negativity raindrops from getting you wet and washing away your drive.

Statistics Aren't Set In Stone

I don't know about you, but being over thirty and single, I am so sick of hearing "all the decent men are taken", "no one wants to commit these days", "it's harder to meet people at this age".

There are so many statistics out there about things like the percentage of people likely to get married within a particular age bracket and how that number drops significantly after you reach a certain age, or how forty per cent of marriages end in divorce. These numbers only become significant in your life when you allow them to affect how you feel.

If you buy into these all studies and believe that they are a real reflection of the world, then you allow them to come into your reality.

Don't forget, what you think about, you bring about. Don't waste your thoughts on silly pointless numbers. Your time will come and it will be worth the wait.

You Do You And I'll Do Me

This is your life, your journey. Don't let anyone get in the way of that. People can feel the need to voice their opinions about your life — sometimes this can be because they care and don't want you to get 'disappointed by failure'. But this can have a negative impact on you and put a strain between you and your end goals.

Remember... the only voice you need to listen to is your own, even if you have people you care about around you telling you what to do and what not to do.

You're on this path for a reason — something that's personal to you, and no one else can understand that like you can.

Thank them for their concern and go on your merry way.

Growth Doesn't Happen Overnight

Diamonds, they really are a girl's best friend. They are beautiful, strong and shine so bright. They are very sought after and have a certain eliteness about them.

But they weren't created overnight.

It takes about one to three and a half billion years for a natural diamond to form.

When you decide to embark on a journey of self-discovery, as eager as you are to get to your goal, don't be disheartened if you feel it's taking too long. Everyone has their own pace and you can't grow overnight.

Anytime you feel like giving up or that you're getting nowhere, remember that you are a diamond and when the time is right, you will shine bright for all the world to see.

You Matter!

Yes you!

Whoever you are, wherever you are, whatever you do, whatever has happened to you and whatever you are going through, you matter.

Don't let anyone tell you otherwise. You have come so far and you have to keep going because you will get to where you want to be.

You are good enough right here, right now and you are worthy of greatness and true happiness.

Don't ever forget how unbelievably amazing you are.

I wish you all the prosperity, love and abundance in the world.

The End